D1519017

LET'S VISIT BURMA

Let's visit
BURMA

AUNG SAN SUU KYI

First published 1985
© Aung San Suu Kyi 1985
All rights reserved. No part of this publication may be reproduced, stored in a retrieval system,
or transmitted, in any form or by any means, electronic, mechanical, photocopying, recording
or otherwise, without the prior permission of Burke Publishing Company Limited.

ACKNOWLEDGEMENTS

The Author and Publishers are grateful to the following organizations and individuals for
permission to reproduce copyright photographs in this book:

Dr. Michael Aris; Camerapix Hutchison Photo Library Ltd; The Mansell Collection
Ltd; MEPhA; Paul Popper Ltd.

CIP data
Aung San Suu Kyi
    Let's visit Burma.
    1. Burma – Social life and customs – Juvenile Literature
    I. Title
    959.1'05   DS527.9

ISBN 0 222 00979 9

Burke Publishing Company Limited
Pegasus House, 116-120 Golden Lane, London EC1Y 0TL, England.
Burke Publishing (Canada) Limited
Registered Office: 20 Queen Street West, Suite 3000, Box 30, Toronto, Canada M5H 1V5.
Burke Publishing Company Inc.
Registered Office: 333 State Street, PO Box 1740, Bridgeport, Connecticut 06601, U.S.A.
Filmset in Baskerville by Graphiti (Hull) Ltd., Hull, England.
Colour reproduction by Swift Graphics (U.K.) Ltd., Southampton, England.
Printed in Singapore by Tien Wah Press (Pte.) Ltd.

915.91
Au 57L

Contents

166950

Zondervan Library
Taylor University
Upland, IN 46989-1022

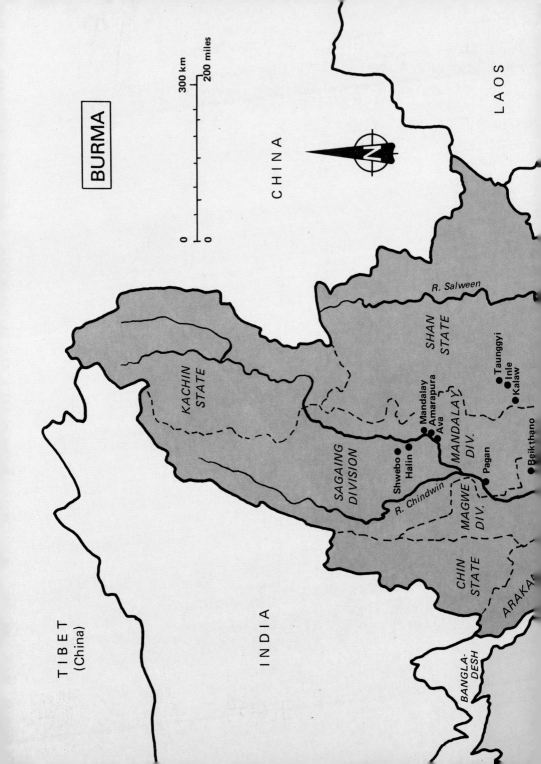

BURMA

300 km
200 miles

TIBET
(China)

CHINA

LAOS

R. Salween

KACHIN
STATE

SHAN
STATE

Taunggyi
Inle
Kalaw

SAGAING
DIVISION

Mandalay
Amarapura
Ava

MANDALAY
DIV.

Shwebo
Halin

Pagan

Beikthano

R. Chindwin

MAGWE
DIV.

INDIA

CHIN
STATE

ARAKAN

BANGLA-
DESH

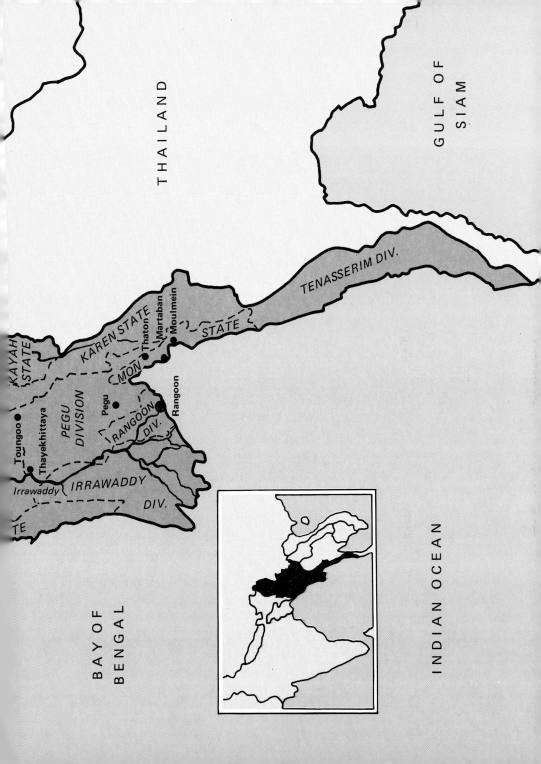

THAILAND

GULF OF SIAM

TENASSERIM DIV.

KAREN STATE

Martaban

Moulmein

Thaton

MON STATE

KAYAH STATE

PEGU DIVISION

Toungoo

Thayekhittaya

Pegu

Rangoon

RANGOON DIV.

Irrawaddy

IRRAWADDY DIV.

TE

BAY OF BENGAL

INDIAN OCEAN

A Wealth of Natural Resources

Burma is one of those countries which seem to have been favoured by nature. Its soil is rich, producing rice and other food crops in abundance. There are vast forests containing a large variety of trees from which valuable timber is extracted.

The ground yields petroleum and many minerals and precious stones including rubies, sapphires and jade. The rivers and streams are full of fish; and from the sea along Burma's coastline come not just seafood but some of the world's loveliest pearls. It is therefore not surprising that Burma has been described as a golden land, an eastern paradise of untold riches. But of course no country on earth is a real paradise and, for all its natural wealth, Burma is not among the rich nations of the world today. It is nevertheless an extremely beautiful country peopled by many different races. It is from the Burmese people, who form the biggest racial group, that the name of the country is derived.

Burma has an area of 676,552 square kilometres (261,218 square miles). To the north is China, to the west India and Bangladesh and to the east Thailand and Laos. The coastline of the Indian Ocean forms a natural boundary to the south. Roughly diamond shaped, Burma is often compared to a kite with a tail trailing along one side.

The main river of Burma is the Irrawaddy which flows from

The Irrawaddy River at Sagaing

the Kachin Hills in the north and follows a southerly course
for over two thousand kilometres (more than one thousand miles)
until it reaches the ocean. Two other rivers of importance are
the Chindwin and the Salween. The Chindwin flows down from
the north-west and joins the Irrawaddy in central Burma. The
Salween comes from a source in the mountains of Tibet and
finds its way across the Shan plateau in eastern Burma down
to the sea.

In the north of Burma are mountains which might be called
the tail end of the eastern Himalayas. The peaks do not rise
to the great height of the mountains further west, but on the

9

border with Tibet is Khakhaporazi reaching 5,887 metres (19,314 feet). Along the north-west border run the Paktai Hills and the Naga Hills. In the west are the Chin Hills, and trailing to the south is the Arakan Yoma (*yoma* is a Burmese term for a ridge of mountains). The Pegu Yoma is another chain of mountains which begins in central Burma and extends down to the Irrawaddy delta.

In the eastern part of the country lies the Shan plateau, a broad tableland averaging between 900 and 1,200 metres (3,000 and 4,000 feet) above sea level.

The plains areas of Burma may be roughly divided into the dry zone in the heart of the country, the coastal lands (Arakan in the west and the long "tail" of Tenasserim in the south-east), and the lush delta of the Irrawaddy.

Administratively, the country is divided into seven states and seven divisions. The seven states represent the homelands of the seven main racial groups, besides the Burmese, who make up the nation: the Chins, Kachins, Karens, Kayahs, Mons, Arakanese (Rakhines) and Shans.

On the whole the climate of Burma is hot and tropical, although the Shan plateau is more temperate. In parts of the Kachin and Chin states, it can be very cold. The monsoon winds, which bring heavy rains for six months of the year, are the most important factor in the seasonal cycle of the country. Instead of spring, summer, autumn and winter, there is the rainy season (from about the middle of May to the middle of October), the cool season (from the end of the rains until about the latter

A view of the Shan plateau in eastern Burma

half of February) and the hot season. The rainfall in an average year varies between about 500 centimetres (200 inches) along the coastlands to between 60 and 115 centimetres (25 and 45 inches) in the dry zone. The temperature also varies across the country but in many parts it rises above 38 degrees Celsius (100 degrees Fahrenheit) during the hot season. The months of December and January are pleasant in the plains with average temperatures between 21 and 26 degrees Celsius (70 and 80 degrees Fahrenheit). On the Shan plateau and in the hill areas it is much colder and there are places where the temperature can fall to freezing-point.

The capital of Burma is Rangoon, a port city on the delta. "Rangoon" is an English corruption of the Burmese name *Yangon,* which means "End of Dangers". This was the name given

11

The Irrawaddy River at
Rangoon, Burma's
capital city

by King Alaungpaya in 1755 to the town built to house the army
with which he vanquished enemy forces in the south. A town
known as Dagon had once flourished on the site of Rangoon,
but by the time of King Alaungpaya, it had dwindled to the
size of a mere hamlet. Rangoon gained importance as a port
town in the eighteenth and nineteenth centuries; and, after
Burma fell to the British in 1885, it became the capital of the
country.

The last capital of the Burmese kings was at Mandalay in
central Burma. Mandalay is not, however, a very old city as
it was founded only in 1857 by King Mindon. The name is taken

12

from a sacred hill near by. According to tradition, the Lord Buddha had prophesied more than two thousand years earlier that a great city would be founded at the foot of the hill. (The Lord Buddha was a north Indian prince whose teachings were to form the basis of one of the world's great religions, Buddhism.) Mandalay has a special place in the hearts of the Burmese, and remains a symbol of the proud days when Burmese kings ruled the country. Unfortunately, the palace of Mandalay was destroyed during the Second World War. Only the walls are left and a few of the gates, topped by graceful pavilions of carved wood. However, there remain other monuments of considerable interest even though not of any great

Lion statues at the foot of Mandalay Hill. It is from this hill that the city of Mandalay, last capital of the Burmese kings, takes its name

The ruins of the royal palace of Mandalay — the walls and some of the graceful gates are all that remain

age. Also around Mandalay are the sites of older royal capitals, Ava and Amarapura.

Moulmein might be termed the third city of Burma. Situated on the Tenasserim coast, it was built up by the British to become the chief town in the territory they acquired in Burma after the first Anglo-Burmese War in 1825. Although it was later displaced by Rangoon as the chief town, Moulmein remained an important urban centre. It is a lively town of brilliant tropical sights, smells and tastes. A popular Burmese saying points out

14

its chief attraction and indicates the outstanding characteristics of the inhabitants of the other two main cities of Burma:

> *Moulmein for food,*
> *Mandalay for conversation,*
> *Rangoon for ostentation.*

Burma is mainly an agricultural country. Its climate and soil, particularly in the rich Irrawaddy delta, are well suited to rice cultivation. At one time Burma exported more rice than any other country in the world. Even today, more than forty per cent of the country's export earnings come from the sale of rice. But it is not merely an export crop. For the people of Burma, rice is the staple food, taken at every main meal. Even in those hill areas where it does not grow so abundantly, the people like to have at least one meal of rice a day.

In the plains of Burma which produce the major rice crops, the wet method of cultivation is used. The fields are kept flooded, either by the rains or, in the drier areas, through a system of irrigation. Sprouting rice seeds are sown in "nursery" fields in April. After about a month, the seedlings—then about thirty centimetres (twelve inches) tall—are transplanted by hand. This is a long, exhausting job, usually undertaken by women. A scene often associated with the Burmese countryside is that of long rows of women bent over flooded rice fields. Songs and dances are based on the transplantation of rice which plays such an important part in the life of the country. The rice is harvested towards the end of the year, again mostly by hand. Modern techniques and farm machinery have been introduced, but traditional methods still prevail.

The most common method of rice cultivation in the hill areas of Burma is that of ''slash and burn'' or shifting cultivation. A plot of land is prepared by cutting down and burning the trees and the scrub. Rain falling on the burnt vegetation enriches the soil on which the rice is planted. After a few years when the soil is exhausted, the plot is abandoned and another one chosen and cleared. The practice of cultivating rice and other food crops in terraced fields is also found in some of the hill areas but it is not as common as the slash and burn method.

The forests of Burma are one of the country's biggest sources of wealth. There are different types of forests, found in many parts of the country. The most important are the mixed deciduous forests which include teak, pyinkado and padauk among the many varieties of valuable trees. The strength, durability and lack of shrinkage of teak makes it one of the most valued woods in the world. Its many uses include shipbuilding, house-building and the making of furniture. Pyinkado is also known as ironwood because of its hardness and strength. It is mainly used for heavy construction work. Padauk has been described as the best all-round utility timber in Burma next to teak. But it means more to the Burmese than just a good wood-producing tree. The blossoms of the padauk, bright yellow and sweetly scented, herald the coming of the rains after months of intense heat. The brave beauty of the flowers which last for only a short time is a popular theme in Burmese poems and songs.

Burma's principal crops apart from rice are sugar-cane, groundnuts, pulses, maize and sesame. Millet, tobacco, cotton and rubber are also produced in considerable quantities. There is a great range of fruit and vegetables in Burma, each season bringing different varieties. Mangoes, bananas, durians, custard apples, mangosteens, water melons and pineapples are some of the tropical fruits which grow abundantly in Burma. The Shan plateau produces oranges, strawberries, avocado pears and other fruit which need a more temperate climate. Tea is one of the most important crops in the northern part of the Shan State. The Burmese not only drink a lot of tea, they also eat the leaves in a pickled form. Coffee is grown in the Chin Hills, where fruits like apples, pears and mulberries are also cultivated. There is such a wealth and variety of agricultural products in Burma that it would need a whole book to describe them all.

The mineral products of Burma are also considerable. Coal, petroleum, natural gas, lead, zinc, tin, wolfram and silver are obtained in quantity. Enough petroleum is produced in central Burma to meet the needs of the whole country. Off-shore oil exploration has not yet produced amounts comparable to the output of the traditional oilfields in the Magwe Division, some of which have been worked for many centuries.

Deposits of coal, silver and lead are found in the Shan State. Other minerals are also mined in varying quantities, but it is for its precious gems that the Shan plateau is famous. Burmese rubies are considered the best in the world and the sapphires too are of an excellent quality. There are also semi-precious stones such as spinel, topaz, zircon and tourmaline. Jadeite and some jade come from the Kachin State. Gold has also been obtained from this northern corner of the country but not in amounts large enough to make it an industry. Zinc mines are concentrated in the Tenasserim Division, and the seabed along the Tenasserim coast is the home of Burmese pearls, the culture of which has been greatly developed in recent years.

Burma's main manufacturing industries are cement, cigarettes, fertilizers, soap, salt and cotton yarn. Most of the manufactured goods are for use within the country but some

Ploughing fields near Mandalay. Burma is an agricultural rather than an industrial nation, and produces a huge variety of crops

A stage in the process of tin mining and refining. Among its many natural resources, Burma has extensive mineral deposits

cement is exported. The major export items, however, are the country's agricultural and natural products: rice, pulses, timber, base metals and silver.

The wealth of Burma's natural resources is impressive, but the great fascination of the country lies in its many peoples with their colourful and diverse origins and customs. It is the histories and civilizations of the peoples of Burma which have built up the character of the nation.

A Turbulent History

The history of Burma might be said to have begun with the arrival of the Mon people from Central Asia, probably between 2500 and 1500 B.C. The Mons settled in parts of Thailand, along the Tenasserim and on the Irrawaddy delta. Indian influences were strong on the early civilization of the Mons. The most important of these influences was perhaps in the area of religion. From India came Hinduism and Buddhism, both of which made an impact on the Mon civilization. Hinduism is the body of beliefs and social practices which developed into the dominant religion of India thousands of years ago. Buddhism developed later, through the teachings of an Indian prince called Siddartha, who was born around 560 B.C. His aim was to help all beings to free themselves from the sufferings of existence. Because he is considered to have rid himself of false beliefs and discovered the path to freedom from suffering, he became known as the Buddha or "Enlightened One".

It is generally accepted that the Mons were predominantly Buddhist from early times. There appears to have been a period when the Mons in Burma came under strong Hindu influence and Buddhism declined. However, by the eleventh century, the Mon kingdoms in Pegu and Thaton are known to have been Buddhist.

The second wave of peoples to come into Burma after the

Mons were the Tibeto-Burmans from the north. The Burmese, who today form the largest racial group in the country, believe that their early Tibeto-Burman ancestors were the Pyus, the Kanyans and the Theks. Little is known about the Kanyans and the Theks beyond their names. Much more can be said of the Pyus who have left traces of a well-developed civilization. In central Burma the site of an ancient Pyu city has been discovered. This city probably dates back to the beginning of the Christian era. Its name, Beikthano, is a Burmese version of the name of the Hindu god, Vishnu. No Buddhist statues or relics have been found here, but there is reason to believe that a type of Buddhism may have existed side by side with the worship of Vishnu.

Other sites of Pyu cities have been excavated at Halin and Thayekhittaya. These are thought to have flourished in the same period, roughly between the fifth and ninth centuries A.D. Halin, like Beikthano, shows no signs of Buddhist statues or relics. However, Buddhist religious objects have been found in Thayekhittaya. Near this city also are three pagodas. These are Buddhist monuments usually built to contain sacred relics. There are many different styles of pagoda and the ones at Thayekhittaya are akin to the ones built in India during the Gupta dynasty which ruled from the fourth to the sixth century A.D.

It is clear that although the Pyus were a Tibeto-Burman people of Mongolian stock, their culture was very similar to that of India. This was a result of Indians coming from the west and

21

One of the pagodas at Thayekhittaya

establishing their rule over the Pyus. For this reason, Burmese tradition has it that the earliest kings of Burma were of princely Indian blood. According to legend, the first kingdom was founded at a place called Tagaung, long before Thayekhittaya or Beikthano. There have not yet been enough archaeological finds to support this legend, but new discoveries in the future may shed more light on the early civilization of the Pyus.

The power of the Pyus appears to have declined in the eighth century. In the ninth century, their kingdom was destroyed by raiders from Nanchao in southern China. From this time the Pyus faded away. Perhaps they moved elsewhere or perhaps they were absorbed by the Burmese who began to make their presence felt at this period. The Burmese were of the same Tibeto-Burman stock as the Pyus. It is not known exactly when they came into Burma or where they lived before they settled in the irrigated areas of the dry zone. However, it is fairly certain that they founded the city of Pagan around A.D. 850.

The name Pagan spells glory and romance for the Burmese. Today the site of the first capital of the Burmese kings is a sun-baked plain studded with thousands of pagodas, most of them in ruins. There are no traces of palaces or great mansions. The people of Pagan have left only religious monuments as a reminder of their glorious dynasty.

Anawratha, who is believed to have ascended the throne of Pagan in 1044, was the first king to establish Burmese rule over

The sun-baked plain of Pagan. It was once the first capital of the Burmese kings. Now, only the ruins of thousands of pagodas and temples remain as a reminder of its former glory

much of the country. He was also the man who did most to promote Theravada Buddhism among the Burmese. "Theravada" means "The Way of the Elders". This is the name applied to the branch of Buddhism which keeps strictly to the teachings of the Lord Buddha as contained in a collection of writings called the *Tripitaka.* Theravada Buddhism is sometimes called "Hinayana", meaning "Small Vehicle", particularly by Buddhists of the Mahayana sect. "Mahayana" means "Great Vehicle". Mahayana Buddhism contains much that is taken from Hinduism and Tantrism, which involves many secret and magic rituals. Mahayana Buddhists tend to believe that their religious practices and attitudes are broader, and therefore greater, than those of the Theravada sect.

There is evidence that both Mahayana and Theravada Buddhism were practised among the Burmese at the time Anawratha became king. It was only after Anawratha's conquest of the Mon kingdom at Thaton, probably between 1054 and 1057, that Theravada Buddhism quickly became the dominant religion. Among the prisoners and rich booty which the victorious Burmese brought back from the Mon country were Theravada monks and religious books. From this time on, the people of Pagan took an increasing interest in religion and became devout Buddhists.

The contacts with the highly civilized Mons contributed greatly towards the development of Burmese culture. Some of the earlier monuments of Pagan were probably built with the help of Mon workmen and artists. It was also during this time

24

A stone plaque in one of the pagodas of Pagan. These plaques, known as Jataka plaques, depict scenes from the Lord Buddha's previous existences

that Burmese began to develop as a written language. Making use of an Indian script, it shows many signs of the influence of the Mon language and of Pali, the language of the Buddhist religious texts.

Anawratha's reign has left a lasting impression on Burma. By bringing the central tract of the country, northern Tenasserim, northern Arakan and some of the western Shan principalities under his sway, he first gave shape to a nation with the three main racial groups under one rule. Theravada Buddhism, which had taken firm root under his patronage, was to be the major factor in forming the character of Burmese society.

In 1077, Anawratha was succeeded by his son Sawlu, a young man who had inherited little of his father's ability. Fortunately his reign was very brief and the throne passed to Kyansittha.

25

A statue of King
Kyansittha, in the
Ananda temple in
Pagan

Kyansittha is one of the most romantic and beloved kings in
Burmese history. His parentage is obscure but he seems to have
been highly born. He had acquired a reputation as a great
general under Anawratha. Towards the end of the king's reign
there was a break in the relations between the two men, but
Kyansittha never turned against Anawratha. It was only in 1084
that Kyansittha ascended the throne, after defeating a force of
Mons who had killed King Sawlu and marched on Pagan.

Kyansittha was not only an outstanding warrior, he was a
king who administered the country well and cared for the welfare
of his subjects. He also did much to promote the cause of

26

religion. The Ananda temple, the most famous of the monuments of Pagan, was built by him.

Pagan was also fortunate in Kyansittha's successor, his grandson Alaungsithu. But no dynasty can continue to produce strong and able rulers for ever. The thirteenth century brought a decline in the quality of the monarchs as well as the rise of powerful forces outside the kingdom. In the north-east, China had come under the rule of the fierce Mongols; and, to the east, the Shans were gaining strength. In 1287, Pagan was sacked by Mongol troops. After that the kingdom built by Anawratha quickly collapsed. The Mons threw off the rule of Pagan, and the Shans swept into central Burma.

The Ananda temple, built by King Kyansittha

The Shans make up the third of the main racial groups of Burma. They belong to the Thai group of peoples who are the most widely distributed in Indo-China. There appear to have been Thai-Shan settlements along the river valleys of South-east Asia since about the eighth century. According to Shan tradition, their first kingdom was set up by Beinnaka, a descendant of the kings of Tagaung after the fall of that ancient Pyu capital. In fact, the name "Tagaung" is thought by some to be a Shan word, which would establish a connection between the Burmese and the Shans from the time of the early Pyus. But that is by no means certain. Shans are first mentioned only in Burmese stone inscriptions of the twelfth century.

In the thirteenth century, new waves of Thai peoples fleeing from the expanding Mongol power came to settle in the eastern plateau of Burma and in present-day Thailand. The Shans of Burma fought back against Mongol domination on the one hand and, on the other, started attacking the tottering kingdom of Pagan.

Between the end of the thirteenth century and the first quarter of the sixteenth century, the Shans dominated central Burma. In the early years after the fall of Pagan, there were three kingdoms ruled by Shan princes. However, by the second half of the fourteenth century, only one of them, Ava, remained as a royal capital. Although the rulers of Ava were of Shan stock, Burmese influences remained strong in the kingdom. Burmese literature flowered during the Ava period, and some of the greatest works in the language were produced at this time. The
28

best known of these are poems with religious themes, composed by Buddhist monks. Buddhism had remained a strong force in the country.

The Mons had thrown off Burmese rule when the power of Pagan weakened. By 1287, a kingdom had been founded at Martaban on the Tenasserim coast by Wareru, a Mon-Shan, who had risen from humble beginnings to become the ruler of lower Burma. Attacks from rising kingdoms in neighbouring Thailand later forced the Mons to abandon Martaban as their capital. They established their new capital in Pegu in 1369.

Pegu was ruled by King Yazadhirit from 1385 to 1423. During his reign, there were repeated wars between the Mons and the kingdom of Ava, ruled by King Minkhaung. The Shan chieftains in the eastern plateau also became involved in the struggles between Pegu and Ava, as did the Arakanese, a people who had founded their kingdom along the western coast of Burma. After the deaths of Yazadhirit and Minkhaung, the fighting between the two kingdoms petered out, especially as Ava was much occupied with trying to keep back ambitious warlike Shan chieftains.

The Mon kingdom flourished in peace and prosperity for several decades. The fifteenth century produced two great rulers, Queen Shin Saw Bu, who reigned from 1453 to 1472, and King Dhammazedi (1472-1492). Both monarchs were devoutly religious and did much to promote the cause of Theravada Buddhism. During their reigns, the Shwedagon pagoda first took on its famous golden magnificence. The Shwedagon stands on

29

a hill in present-day Rangoon. Its name means "Golden Dagon". Dagon is the name of the Mon settlement which had once existed on the site of Rangoon. The Shwedagon is most sacred and most dear to the people of Burma. There are many legends surrounding the great pagoda. According to tradition, the original monument was built during the lifetime of the Buddha himself. This cannot be verified but there certainly had been a monument there, believed to contain sacred relics of the Lord Buddha since early times. Stone inscriptions set up by Dhammazedi tell the story of how the pagoda was built up and embellished by successive monarchs of Pegu. The Shwedagon is a lasting memorial to the devotion of the Mons to the Buddhist faith.

A general view of Rangoon, with the magnificent Shwedagon pagoda, covered with layers of solid gold leaf and crowned by a jewelled orb

Worshippers at the Shwethalyaung, a huge image of the Lord Buddha reclining on his side

In Pegu itself, there are two other famous monuments much revered by Buddhists. These are the Shwemawdaw pagoda and the Shwethalyaung. The second is a huge, beautiful image of the Lord Buddha reclining on his side. It is about 55 metres (180 feet) long and 16 metres (52 feet) high. The Shwemawdaw pagoda is supposed to contain among its sacred relics two hairs from the head of the Lord Buddha. Both the Shwemawdaw and the Shwethalyaung were built before the reign of King Dhammazedi, but he maintained them well and also built other religious monuments.

31

Burma's first contacts with the west were made during the fifteenth century. Italian merchants were the first to trade with the Mon kingdom but the Portuguese who came later were to play a bigger role in the affairs of Burma. The Portuguese established colonies in India and on the Malay Peninsula during the early years of the sixteenth century. A trading-station was opened at the Mon settlement of Martaban and trade began between the Mons and the Portuguese.

The years of Pegu's stability were also the years of Ava's decline. The kings of Ava were unable to hold out against the Shan chieftains, who interfered more and more in the affairs of the kingdom. As Ava fell into chaos, the power of Toungoo began to rise.

Toungoo was a city some four hundred kilometres (two hundred and fifty miles) south of Ava. Many Burmese had taken refuge there after the fall of Pagan. Throughout the Ava dynasty, Toungoo remained a sanctuary for Burmese wishing to escape from the persecution of some of the Shan kings. In 1486, Minkyinyo came to the throne of Toungoo and Burmese power began to revive.

The Toungoo period is known as the Second Unification of Burma (the first was under Anawratha of Pagan). Minkyinyo's son, Tabinshwehti, (who reigned from 1531 to 1550) succeeded to the throne at only fourteen years of age. But he was a great warrior as well as a considerable statesman. During his reign, the Mon country and much of central Burma came under Burmese rule. Tabinshwehti made his capital at Pegu. He seems

32

to have liked the Mons and to have admired their culture. He spent most of his life waging wars, carrying out repeated compaigns against Thailand. He also led an expedition to the Arakanese kingdom. Many Portuguese were involved in these wars. They served as paid soldiers under the Burmese, the Thais and the Arakanese. They also introduced firearms from Europe.

Tabinshwehti was murdered at the age of thirty-two by one of his Mon subjects. During his last days he had become a drunkard under the influence of a Portuguese favourite. Much of the care of the Burmese kingdom had therefore become the responsibility of Bayinnaung. Bayinnaung means "Elder Brother of the King", and this was the title Tabinshwehti had conferred on the man who was his best general, his most trusted adviser and also his brother-in-law. At Tabinshwehti's death it seemed for a time as if the young Burmese kingdom would fall to pieces. But Bayinnaung not only managed to hold it together, he built it up to greater size and strength.

Bayinnaung brought the Burmese, the Shans and the Mons under one rule. He also established his overlordship on some of the neighbouring provinces of Thailand. Pegu became a wealthy capital and a well-known trading-centre. However, after the death of Bayinnaung, the state began to crumble. He had a number of able successors, but the kingdom was too large for them to be able to retain control. Troubles came from the Thais and the Arakanese. Lower Burma became a battleground for the warring armies.

The country was already exhausted from the wars of

33

166950

ZONDERVAN LIBRARY
Taylor University
500 W Reade Avenue
Upland IN 46989-1001

Tabinshwehti and Bayinnaung. Rich ricelands remained untilled and turned to jungle. Without Bayinnaung's strong personality to keep them in check, the Portuguese started playing a more prominent role in the quarrels between the Burmese, the Arakanese and the Thais. At one time De Brito, a Portuguese who had served as a gunner under the king of Arakan, became governor of the port town of Syriam and made a bid to establish his authority over lower Burma. He was eventually defeated and executed by the Burmese king but, as one trouble was put down, another arose.

In 1635, the Burmese kings moved their capital to Ava. The following century brought a tangle of troubles with the Shans, the Chinese, the Thais, the Mons and the Indian border state of Manipur. A rebellion started in lower Burma in 1740. In 1752 a force of Mons burnt Ava and took the king prisoner. The Toungoo dynasty had come to an end.

The year Ava was burnt down was also the year of the rise of a new Burmese dynasty. Aung Zeya, the headman of a village near Shwebo in central Burma, rallied the Burmese to his standard. He was to become known as Alaungpaya, the first king of the Konbaung dynasty. During a short reign of eight years, he brought the Burmese, the Shans and the Mons once more under one rule. He also extended his powers to some of the outlying provinces of Thailand. The years from 1752 to 1760 brought the third unification of Burma.

The Konbaung dynasty saw ten kings and four capitals: Shwebo, from where Alaungpaya had begun his rise to kingship,

A ruined pagoda at Amarapura. Amarapura, founded in 1783, was one of the four capitals of the Konbaung dynasty

Ava, the old capital, Amarapura, founded in 1783, and finally Mandalay, last city of the Burmese kings. The first Konbaung kings were strong and warlike. Arakan was brought into the Burmese kingdom. Manipur and Assam on the Indian border became vassal states. There were also many wars with the Thais. But the old pattern of neighbouring kingdoms fighting for supremacy had been altered by the coming of the Europeans.

During the seventeenth and eighteenth centuries the Portuguese, the Dutch, the French and the British all scrambled for trading rights and possessions in South and South-east Asia. India came under British domination. It was the era of colonial expansion. Relations between the Burmese and the British were stormy from the beginning. There had been clashes even during

35

the reign of Alaungpaya. However, it was only in 1824 that the first Anglo-Burmese War broke out, over Manipur and Assam. The Burmese could not hold out against the modern military equipment of the British. As a result of the defeat, Burma had to give up its claims to Manipur and Assam. The provinces of Arakan and Tenasserim also had to be surrendered to the British. Relations between the Burmese and the British did not improve and a second war broke out in 1852. The Burmese once again got the worst of it and the whole of lower Burma fell under British rule. Yet another war broke out in 1885. This one was decisive, for British troops marched on Mandalay and captured the Burmese royal family. Thibaw, the last of the Konbaung kings, was taken away to India; and Burma was made a part of the British Empire.

A contemporary sketch of King Thibaw, the last Burmese king, being taken away by the British in 1885

Building an Independent Nation

British rule brought many changes to Burma. The boundaries of the country were drawn along lines which have remained practically unchanged to the present day. Burma was administered as a province of British India. The rich natural resources of the country were developed and the economy prospered. But British policy also brought in large numbers of Indians and Chinese. These immigrants were hard-working and skilled at business. The new wealth of the country passed into their hands and into those of the British companies rather than to the people of Burma. There was no real contact between the colonial rulers and their subjects.

Pockets of Burmese resistance flared up in different parts of the country after the fall of Mandalay. The British brought in tens of thousands of troops from India to put down the uprisings. They succeeded to a large measure in bringing peace to the countryside. However, the Burmese did not become reconciled to foreign domination. The British found it easier to deal with some of the other racial groups. The Christian missionaries who had come in large numbers also found it easier to convert those peoples of Burma who were not already staunch Buddhists. They were particularly successful with the Karens along the south-eastern tract of Burma. The practice of encouraging the differences between the various racial groups was to have sad consequences for the independent nation of the future.

Burmese nationalism began to gather strength again in the 1920s. It started as a movement to keep the Buddhist religion pure in the face of foreign influences. Later the movement became more political in character. In 1930 there was an uprising of the peasants led by a man called Saya San. The rebellion was quickly stamped out but other nationalist movements continued. In 1937, Burma was separated from India under the British administration. A new constitution came into effect. Under its provisions the people of Burma were given a bigger role to play in the running of their country. But this was not enough to stem the tide of nationalism.

During the 1930s, the students of Rangoon University had become prominent in nationalist activities. Some of the student leaders went on to become members of a political organization called the *Dohbama Asiayone. (Dohbama* means ''We Burmese'' and *Asiayone* means ''Association''.) They became known as *thakins* (which means ''masters'') because they used this word as a prefix to their names. It was the word the Burmese had to use when addressing their British rulers. The young *thakins* wanted to make it clear that the Burmese should be their own masters. Nationalist activities increased and became more militant.

The beginning of the Second World War in 1939 was a turning-point for the Burmese independence movement. Nationalist politicians urged the people not to support British war efforts unless Burma was promised independence at the end of the war. The British government arrested many nationalists. A group of young men left the country secretly to receive military training in Japan. They came to be known as the ''Thirty Comrades''. Japan was a strong and independent nation. Since it had defeated Russia at war in the beginning of the twentieth century, it had been admired by other Asian countries. The Burmese hoped that the Japanese would help them win back their independence. The Burma Independence Army was organized with the ''Thirty Comrades'' as the nucleus. In 1941, it marched into Burma with the Japanese. The British were driven out of the country.

Burma was declared an independent nation. In fact, the country had simply exchanged one foreign ruler for another.

Japanese soldiers marching through the town of Moulmein in 1942. The Japanese army and the Burma Independence Army joined forces to drive the British out of the country

The occupying Japanese army began to treat the Burmese like a subject people. Burmese people were put in all the key positions of government and administration. In that sense they gained a degree of self-government. But the Japanese had the final authority.

The commander-in-chief of the Burmese army was a young man called Aung San who had been a student leader and one of the "Thirty Comrades". Together with other nationalists, he organized a resistance movement against the Japanese. The tide of the war began to turn. British troops came back to Burma and, as the Burmese army had risen against the Japanese, the British and the Burmese now fought on one side. The Japanese were defeated and the war in Burma came to an end in 1945.

British troops landing at Rangoon in 1945. Shortly after this, the Japanese were defeated and the war in Burma came to an end

Aung San (*right*), leader of the Anti-Fascist People's Freedom League, and U Nu, the party's vice-president

However, this was not the end of Burma's struggle for independence. The Burmese did not want the British to come back as their rulers. The strongest opponent of British rule was the Anti-Fascist People's Freedom League (AFPFL), a nationalist party led by Aung San who had left the army to engage in independence politics. The British gradually had to give in to the demands of the AFPFL, which had won the popular support of the country. But, while agreeing to Burmese demands for independence, the British insisted that the peoples along the frontiers of Burma (the Kachins from the north, the Chins from the north-west and the Shans) should be allowed to decide their own future for themselves. It was thought by some of the British that the frontier peoples would not wish to

41

throw in their lot with the Burmese. However, the Burmese leaders managed to win the confidence of the Shans, Chins and Kachins. They decided to co-operate with the Burmese in the movement for independence. The British had no choice but to hand the government of Burma back to its people.

Before Burma formally became an independent nation, Aung San and six of his ministers were assassinated at a cabinet meeting by gunmen sent by a political rival. Aung San was only thirty-two years old. He is considered the national hero of Burma and the father of the nation.

Burma became an independent republic on 4th January 1948. U Nu, the most senior member of the AFPFL remaining after the assassinations, became the first prime minister. The young nation was immediately faced with grave problems. Burmese communists had worked for independence with the AFPFL, but some of them felt that the cause of international communism came before national interests. They started armed rebellions against the AFPFL government. The People's Volunteer Organization, which had been organized in case it was necessary to fight the British for independence, but which was scheduled to be disbanded, also took up arms. The third group of rebels was the Karen National Defence Organization. In the past there had been clashes between the Burmese and the Karens. Many Karens were Christians and religious differences served to widen the gap between the two peoples. Aung San and other Burmese nationalists had worked hard to bring about better relations. Although they managed to win the trust of some Karens, others

42

The independence monument in Rangoon

refused to believe that it was possible to live in peace under a Burmese government. Some Burmese attitudes have been responsible for the distrust of the Karens. But the British and the missionaries who worked among the Karens must also bear the blame for the division between the two peoples.

On gaining independence, Burma became a parliamentary democracy. The government managed to hold out against the rebellions, and a fair measure of peace was restored. However, the need to keep the rebels in check made the army strong. Many of the top men in the army had been politicians and were inclined to interfere in the government of the country. In 1962, a group

43

of army officers led by Ne Win, the commander-in-chief, overthrew the elected government of U Nu. Since then, Burma has been under army rule, although many officers in high government posts have laid aside their military titles.

Burma under army rule became a socialist republic, guided by the Burmese Socialist Programme Party. No other political party is permitted. This, and other measures limiting the political liberties of the people, are aimed at creating a stable government and a united country. But unity can come only with the willing co-operation of the people. The government of Burma still has to cope with many rebels, prominent among them Karens, Shans and communists. The economy has not been well managed and Burma today is not a prosperous nation. However, with its wealth of natural resources, there is always hope for the future. And that future lies in the hands of its peoples.

The Minority Peoples of Burma

There are a great many peoples in Burma, speaking over one hundred languages. However, each of these peoples belongs to one of three major racial groups, the Mon-Khmers, the Tibeto-Burmans and the Thai-Shans. The seven peoples, apart from the Burmese, who are numerous enough to have separate administrative states marked out for them in the country are the Chins, Kachins, Karens, Kayahs, Mons, Arakanese (Rakhines) and Shans.

The Chins live in the hilly north-western part of Burma. They belong to the Tibeto-Burman racial group. There are many separate tribes and districts among the Chins. This is due to the nature of the area they live in, which does not make for easy communication. The best-known groups, named according to the areas where they live, are the Tidam Chins, the Falam Chins and the Hakha Chins. Some Chin peoples call themselves *Zo-mi*, or *Lai-mi*. Both terms mean "Mountain People".

The Chins live by agriculture. They use the "slash and burn" method for planting rice and other food crops. This has led to the clearing of some of the thick forests which covered the Chin Hills. They are skilled at hunting and fishing. Traditionally, domestic animals were reared mainly to be used as sacrifices

45

in religious ceremonies. The mithan, a kind of cow, is particularly valued.

In the old days, all the Chins were spirit-worshippers. Now there are some Christians and Buddhists among them. Among the Tidam and Hakha Chins are some followers of the Pau Chin Hau religion. Pau Chin Hau was born in the Tidam area in 1859 and lived until 1948. He started a religious movement based on the worship of a god known as Pasian. He also invented a script. Originally, the Chins had no written language. Today, apart from the Pau Chin Hau system, there is also a written Chin language using the Roman alphabet.

There are many feasts and festivals among the Chins, differing from area to area: seasonal festivals, agricultural festivals and feasts concerned with the worship of spirits and ancestors. Perhaps the most interesting of them all is the *Khhaung Cawi*. This is a feast given by a man to honour his wife. Up to one hundred mithan may be killed during one of these feasts, which go on for seven days. On the last day, the wife of the host is lifted on to the *Khhaung,* a swinging bamboo platform, to scatter gifts. Only a wealthy man could afford such a feast.

In some parts of the Chin Hills, the women tattoo their faces. The patterns vary according to the tribe. Some can be quite elaborate while others are just a few well-placed dots. The most distinctive feature of Chin dress is the woven blanket which is draped around the body. Thick, smooth cotton patterned with broad stripes, these blankets have become a very popular item of bedding for people all over Burma.

46

Chin women with tattoes on their faces

The Chins make ornaments of bronze and copper. They are also skilled at weaving mats and baskets from split cane. Some of the finest examples of their craftsmanship can be seen in the carved columns of wood and stone which they raise as memorials to the dead.

The Kachins of Burma are another Tibeto-Burman people. The inhabitants of the Kachin State can be divided into four main language groups—the Jingpaws, Marus, Yaywins and Lisus. Towards the end of the nineteenth century, Christian missionaries developed a written form of Jingpaw, using the Roman alphabet. Because of this, Jingpaw became the most

47

widely known of the languages in the Kachin State. When people speak of Kachins, they usually mean the Jingpaw group. The other groups are not so widely known, partly because their numbers are less.

Most of the Kachins traditionally worshipped spirits, although Christians and Buddhists can now be found among them. There are many spirits, but there is one supreme being who rules over all others, called Karai Kasang. Only live animals are sacrificed to him. These sacrificial animals are allowed to live free and unharmed. Perhaps the most powerful of the other spirits is the *Madai* spirit, from whom the Kachin *duwas* (chieftains) are thought to be descended. It is mainly in his honour that the *manao* feast, the most important celebration among the Kachins,

Kachin women weaving

is held. Different types of *manao* feasts are held for different reasons. For example, they may celebrate a victory in battle, mark the occasion of an elderly person's death, or may be an occasion for inviting the *Madai* spirit to a new territory.

Only *duwas* (chieftains) may sacrifice to the *Madai* spirit. Therefore *manao* feasts may only be given by *duwas*. In any case, the expense of such feasts would be beyond most ordinary people. A great *manao* requires about a year's preparation. Four *manao* columns, painted red, black and white, are set up in a chosen field, together with poles to which the sacrificial animals are tethered. Many little shrines for spirits are built around the field. (Although a *manao* is held chiefly for the *Madai* spirit, sacrifices are made to others as well.)

There is much eating, drinking and dancing during a *manao* feast. A big double-sided drum and a large brass gong boom out the traditional sounds of *manao*. The original *manao* dance imitates birds, with the dancers holding fans which represent the outspread tail of a peacock. The Kachins have many dances in which both men and women take part. There are dances depicting horse-riding, the casting of fishing-nets, the search for scattered cattle. There are also dances for funerals, performed to the sound of cracked gongs.

The Kachins have three kinds of traditional government. The one found mostly in the northern areas is called *gumyao-gumsa*. This is a kind of democracy where each community is ruled according to the will of the majority.

Gumhsa is the system most common to the Jingpaw speaking

areas. Here the authority is in the hands of land-owning hereditary *duwas*. There are two classes of *duwas*—those who are entitled to one leg of each game animal killed by their subjects and those who are not so privileged. The most highly esteemed *duwas* are those who are descended from a line of youngest sons. Among the Kachins, it is the youngest, not the eldest, who is the heir.

The third system of traditional government among the Kachins is *gumlao*. This may perhaps be described as a revolutionary system of government. It exists in the areas around Hukawng valley, where the people had revolted against the authority of the *duwas* and established a system of electing headmen by popular choice. These revolutions are thought to have taken place some three to four hundred years ago. In some areas, *gumlao* was introduced later. Under the British, some of the *gumlao* areas reverted back to the *gumhsa* system of hereditary *duwas*.

The Kachins are a handsome people. The men look very dashing in their traditional turbans and baggy trousers, with curved swords dangling at their sides. The women are striking in their costumes heavily decorated with silver ornaments. The Lisus, Marus and Yaywins also have their own different costumes. The Lisu women are considered to be particularly attractive.

The origins of the Karens have been a matter for much discussion. Some Christian missionaries have even thought they might be descendants of a lost tribe of Israel. It was also believed for a long time that the Karens were a Thai-Shan people. However, studies of their languages and social customs have given convincing proof that they belong to the Tibeto-Burman group. There are several different kinds of Karens, such as the Pao, the Sagaw and the Bwe.

The Karens, like the Chins and the Kachins, were traditionally spirit-worshippers. Today there are many Christians among them and some Buddhists. In addition, there

A girl from the Kachin State in her traditional costume

A woman from the Karen State

are a number of other religious groups which are peculiar to the Karens. One of the most interesting is that which follows the *Lèkè* faith. This is a kind of Buddhism based on the worship of Maitreya, the Buddha who will next appear in this world. However, unlike other Buddhists, their faith does not include the worship of sacred images, pagodas or monks. Their principal religious monument is a wooden structure without walls. In the centre is a tall pole bearing a sacred umbrella. The people of the *Lèkè* faith abide by ten rules of conduct which seem to reflect Buddhist ideas.

The religion which has undoubtedly had the greatest impact

52

on Karen life is Christianity. The missionaries who converted the people also gave them schools and education. This enabled many Karens to go on to higher studies and take up modern professions. Karen women have acquired a reputation as excellent hospital nurses. They are also much sought after as nannies.

Like most of the peoples of Burma, the Karens have traditionally lived by agriculture. They are also known as expert foresters. Karens are particularly skilled at capturing and taming wild elephants. They train the elephants to work with heavy logs in the timber camps. Karens depend on patience and perseverence to train the animals. They do not use cruel methods.

Spirit-worship still exists among the Karens. The devout Christians frown upon this. Buddhists are generally more tolerant, but some of them are also strongly opposed to spirit-worship. A traditional Karen occasion where peoples of different religions can gather together is the ''Shouting Feast'', as it is known to the Burmese. This is really arranged for young people in the villages to get to know each other. Two rows of girls sit facing one another and the young men parade between the rows, stripped to their waists, to show that they are healthy and well-formed. Later the young men take part in wrestling matches. Then they have an exchange of poems and songs with the girls. This is a kind of competition of wit and knowledge. It is because these exchanges are usually made loudly and clearly that the Burmese have named the occasion a ''Shouting Feast''.

Karens are good singers and many of them have beautiful voices. They have their own dances and musical instruments. Their bronze drums, known as "frog drums" because of the little figures of frogs cast on them, are well known and very valuable.

The Kayah State adjoins the Karen State. It is a beautiful area with hills and many waterfalls. A big hydroelectric project has been set up at the Lawpita Falls. The Kayah people used to be known as Karennis (Red Karens) because of the colour of their costumes. There are a number of different peoples within the state. Perhaps the best known among them are the Padaung, whose women are often called "giraffe women". This is because of their long necks stretched by putting on row upon row of thick brass rings from the time they are about ten, increasing the number over the years. Many of the women wear twenty or more rings.

Situated between the Shans and the Karens, some similarities to both peoples can be seen in the customs and traditions of the Kayahs. Their traditional chieftains are called *saopya* (Shan chieftains are called *saopha*). The area was originally divided under the rule of five *saopyas*, but two of the lines died out before the Second World War. As in the Shan State, these rulers have now surrendered their hereditary rights and privileges.

The "frog drum", so valued by the Karens, is equally valued by the Kayah people. The music of the drum is only for joyful occasions. There are other musical instruments, including gongs,

54

A tribal girl at a market in the Kayah State

drums and wind instruments, some made of buffalo horn. Among the songs of the Kayah people are those called È-*yoe,* which have been handed down from generation to generation. They tell of events which have taken place since the beginning of the world. A careful study of the È-*yoe* songs could reveal more information about the origins and history of the people.

Among the Kayah people, as among the Karens, traditional spirit-worship has been replaced to some extent by Christianity and Buddhism. However, the most important festival of the year is the *Kuhtobo* festival, dedicated to the spirit responsible for rain

55

and good weather. In the old days this festival was celebrated at a district level, but since independence it has become a state occasion. The *Kuhtobo* festival is centred on sacrificing to the spirits and raising a sacred pole. It is a time for feasting and joy and takes place around May.

The history and civilization of the Mons have already been discussed in some detail. In spite of the many years of warfare between the two peoples, the Mons and the Burmese have mixed freely and intermarried. Today they are indistinguishable from each other except for the slight and rather attractive accent with which some Mons speak Burmese.

The Arakanese on the western coast of Burma have a long history which can compare with that of the Mons and the Burmese. However, because the area is cut off from the rest of Burma by the Arakan Yoma, the Arakanese have not been so closely involved in the wars of the other two peoples. Powerful kings from central Burma have made their authority felt in Arakan, invading it and demanding tribute. But it was only in the eighteenth century that it was annexed to the Burmese kingdom by King Bodawpaya.

   The early peoples of Arakan are something of a mystery. It is thought that they were a mixture of Mongolian and Aryan peoples who had come over from India. Certainly the early kings of Arakan were of Indian stock. There are now several groups of peoples in the Arakan State: Arakanese, Thek, Dainet, Myo,

Mramagyi and Kaman. The Arakanese are Tibeto-Burmans and their language is very close to Burmese. In fact, some regard it as archaic Burmese. The languages of some of the other groups show the influence of Bengali. Because of its geographical position, Bengal has played a major part in the history and civilization of Arakan. In the fifteenth century, Bengal helped the Arakanese to resist the power of the kings of Ava. From then on, the kings of Arakan used Islamic titles, although they and the majority of their subjects remained Buddhist. However, there are more people of the Islamic faith to be found in Arakan than anywhere else in Burma.

Despite these Bengali and Islamic influences, however, Arakan has been a predominantly Buddhist region for centuries. According to tradition, Buddhism came to the western coast of Burma during the lifetime of the Buddha. This cannot be verified, but the most famous image of the Buddha made by the Arakanese is thought to date back to the second century A.D. This image, the Maha Myamuni, was taken away by King Bodawpaya's son when he conquered Arakan. It is considered one of the most sacred images in the country and is now enshrined in Mandalay. The loss of their great image was a deep sorrow to the Arakanese. There are those who say that the real Maha Myamuni could never have been taken out of Arakan and that it lies hidden somewhere in its jungles.

There are many pagodas and Buddhist temples in Arakan. Many of their religious festivals are Buddhist festivals, similar to the ones celebrated by the Burmese, and there are many

A street scene in Akyab, the capital of Arakan state

similarities between the two peoples. There is, however, one Arakanese custom which is very alien to the Burmese. The Arakanese favour marriage between cross cousins. (Children of one's mother's brothers or of one's father's sisters are known as cross cousins.) This is a reflection of Islamic influence.

There are many fine examples of Arakanese literature. A poem by an Arakanese courtier of the fifteenth century, known as the "Arakanese Princess E-gyin" is one of the first examples of the *e-gyin* type of poetry. After Arakan came under British rule in 1826, English became the language of the educated and Arakanese literature declined.

Today one of the greatest attractions of Arakan for people from all over Burma as well as for tourists is its beautiful beaches.

58

The Shan plateau is looked upon by the Burmese as a beautiful, romantic land. With its temperate climate, lakes and hills, it is certainly a most attractive part of the country. The Shans, as already mentioned, have played a very active part in the history of Burma. There are many different peoples in the area marked out as the Shan State. The majority belong to the Thai-Shan group like the Shans themselves, but there are also those who fall within the Tibeto-Burman and the Mon-Khmer groups. It is estimated that there are twenty-seven major sub-groups, including the Shans, Pa-o, Palaung, Kachin, Intha and Danu. In addition there are thirty-two lesser known tribes.

Under the kings of Burma there were nine Shan States whose rulers (known as *saophas*) were given the right to use the five symbols of kingship: white umbrella, royal headdress, yak-hair swish, royal slippers and royal dagger. There were also other

A young girl and baby in a Palaung village in the Shan State

principalities on the Shan plateau. Under the British there were thirty-seven administrative divisions, the biggest ones ruled by *saophas* and the others under the authority of *myosas* (governors) or *ngwegunmhus* (excise officers). After independence, in 1959, the *saophas* signed an agreement giving up their hereditary rights and privileges.

Of all the minority peoples of Burma, the Shans are probably best known to foreigners today. This is partly because of the size of their territory and partly because parts of the Shan State are included in those areas open to tourists.

The Inle lake is a great tourist attraction. The people, called Intha, live off the lake, fishing and cultivating gardens on the floating islands produced by a mixture of silt and water weeds. A peculiarity about the Intha boatmen is that they row their boats standing up with one leg hooked around the oar to pull it. Other places which tourists may visit in the Shan State are Taunggyi, the state capital, and Kalaw, a well-known hot-weather resort.

Silk woven at Inle is popular with women all over Burma. Another Shan product known and used everywhere in the country is the woven bag which can be slung over the shoulders. It would be a very unusual Burmese household that did not have one of these colourful bags, for men, women and children all use them. Tea and pickled tea-leaves are also among the chief products exported from the Shan State to the rest of the country.

Within driving distance from Kalaw are the Pindaya caves, a series of caverns which contain many images of the Buddha,

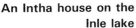
An Intha house on the Inle lake

of different sizes. It is a strange and awesome place with beautiful images suddenly coming into sight around dark corners.

Spirit-worship is practised by some of the Shans as well as by other peoples on the plateau. Christians are also found among some of the tribal groups. As most of the Shans are Buddhists, their main festivals mark important days of the Buddhist calendar.

In recent years much publicity has been given to the area of the Shan State which falls within the "Golden Triangle". This is the name given to the junction where Burma, Laos and Thailand meet. It is an area where opium poppies are grown

61

Opium poppies growing in the "Golden Triangle". Heroin, one of the most dangerous drugs in the world, is derived from opium

in vast quantities. One of the most dangerous drugs of today, heroin, is derived from opium. The growing addiction to heroin among people in America and western Europe has made it very valuable. However, the poor farmers who grow opium poppies do not get rich. It is the people who smuggle heroin in large quantities to the western countries who make large profits. Some of the people who grow opium also become addicted to it. However, as they do not take it in a highly concentrated and refined form, the effects are not as disastrous as among heroin addicts who inject the drug into their bodies. Attempts are being

62

made by several governments to control the opium trade. This is not easy, however, as the "Golden Triangle" covers difficult terrain, parts of it often overrun by rebels.

Apart from the many indigenous racial groups of Burma, Indian and Chinese immigrants must be mentioned among its minority peoples. Under British rule there was no control on the numbers of Indians and Chinese who came to seek their fortune in Burma. Many Indians left the country during the advance of the Japanese during the Second World War, although some came back after the war was over. Indians and Chinese also left Burma after it became an independent nation. However, there are still large numbers of Indian and Chinese people, particularly in the towns and cities.

Some of the Indians and Chinese have intermarried with the local peoples. For many, Burma is the only home they have ever known and they love it as their own country. There are others whose loyalties to the countries of their origin and to their own people are still strong. In the past there have been serious clashes between the Burmese and the immigrant communities. On the whole, though, they have all lived together peacefuly.

The many peoples of Burma make it a fascinating country, rich in variety and tradition. Among them, the Burmese form the majority. It is therefore their habits and customs which have come to be most often associated with Burma.

The Burmese

The one single factor which has had the most influence on Burmese culture and civilization is Theravada Buddhism. In all parts of the country where the Burmese people live there are pagodas and Buddhist monasteries. The graceful tapering shape of a pagoda, painted white or gilded to a shining gold, is a basic part of any Burmese landscape. Burma is often called the "Land of Pagodas".

Buddhism teaches that suffering is an unavoidable part of existence. At the root of all suffering are such feelings as desire, greed and attachment. Therefore to be free from suffering it is necessary to be free from those undesirable feelings. This freedom can be obtained by following the Noble Eightfold Path:

Right Understanding
Right Thought
Right Speech
Right Action
Right Livelihood
Right Effort
Right Mindfulness
Right Concentration

This path is also known as the Middle Way, because it avoids
64

two extremes: one extreme is the search for happiness through the pursuit of pleasure, the other extreme is the search for happiness through inflicting pain on oneself. The final goal of a Buddhist is to be liberated from the cycle of existence and rebirth, called *samsara.* Once this final liberation is achieved, one may be said to have attained *nirvana;* this word means "extinction" and might be explained as Ultimate Reality for all Buddhists.

The teachings of the Buddha are known as the Dharma, and these teachings are generally passed on to ordinary people by the Buddhist monks, collectively known as the Sangha. Therefore, the Buddha, the Dharma and the Sangha are called the "Triple Gem". Because the Lord Buddha was a great teacher, the Burmese have a great reverence for all teachers. Parents are also regarded with "awe, love and respect". Consequently, the Triple Gem, teachers and parents make up the "five that must be revered" by Burmese Buddhists.

All good Buddhists undertake to abide by the Five Precepts: not to take life, not to steal, not to commit adultery, not to tell lies, not to take intoxicating drinks. Although the taking of life is considered such an evil that many Burmese will go out of their way to avoid stepping on an insect, there are few who avoid eating meat. This is considered inconsistent by some people. The Burmese would probably argue that the Lord Buddha himself ate meat. The Burmese are a practical people. They have also been described as happy-go-lucky.

As might be expected, many Burmese festivals are based on

Offering water to an image of the Lord Buddha at the base of the Sunday planetary post in the Shwedagon pagoda

Buddhist events. Festival days are determined by the Burmese calendar, which is calculated according to the phases of the moon. The full moon days of the month of *Kason* (April/May), *Waso* (June/July) and *Thidingyut* (October/November) are special days for the Buddhists. The full moon day of *Kason* celebrates the birth, enlightenment and death of the Buddha. The Buddha achieved enlightenment—that is, he finally shed all false beliefs and saw through to the ultimate truth—underneath a *bodhi* tree. On the full moon of *Kason,* therefore, people pour offerings of water on *bodhi* trees.

The full moon day of *Waso* also celebrates important events in the life of the Buddha, in particular the first sermon he preached on the truth he had learnt. In addition, this day marks
66

the beginning of the ''Buddhist Lent'', which lasts for three months. During this time the monks are not allowed to travel. Many Buddhists observe what are known as the ''eight precepts'' on all the holy days during Lent. The Buddhist holy days are the day of the dark moon, the eighth day of the new moon, the day of the full moon and the eighth day after the full moon. The eight precepts are four of the basic five precepts (not to kill, steal, lie or take intoxicating drinks) with the addition of four others: not to commit any immoral acts, not to take any food after twelve noon, not to indulge in music, dancing and the use of perfume, not to sleep in high places. (The last is taken to mean that one should not sleep in a luxurious bed.) Some devout Buddhists keep these eight precepts throughout the three months of Lent. Because it is a time when people should be thinking of their spiritual development, Buddhists should not get married during this period. Marriage brings family life and therefore greater ties and attachments. Thus it is likely to make the achieving of *nirvana* more difficult.

The end of Lent coincides with the end of the monsoon rains in October. It is a time for happiness and rejoicing. Tradition has it that the Lord Buddha spent one Lent in the *Tavatimsa* heaven to preach to his mother. (His mother had died in giving birth to him and had been reborn in *Tavatimsa,* one of the many Buddhist heavens.) At the end of Lent, he came back to earth and the people of the world welcomed him with lights. In celebration of this, during the three days of the *Thidingyut* festival, pagodas, monasteries and homes are decorated with lights and lanterns. Cities like Rangoon and Mandalay are ablaze with coloured lights, and there are competitions to see which part of the town is the most beautifully decorated. *Thidingyut* is a time for expressing reverence towards older people. Many Burmese visit older friends and relatives to bow down before them and to offer gifts.

There are other Buddhist festivals apart from the ones described above. In addition, many pagodas have their own festival day. One of the most important pagoda festivals is that of the great Shwedagon in Rangoon, which takes place in March. Soaring to a height of almost one hundred metres (over three hundred feet), covered with layers of solid gold leaf and topped with a hollow gold orb encrusted with many precious gems, the Shwedagon is the most famous landmark in the country. Foreigners come to look at it with curiosity and wonder. For the Burmese it is not just an interesting and beautiful monument, but a very central part of their religious life—and not just on festival days. Every day, an endless stream of people climb up to the Shwedagon from one of its four great stairways (an electric lift has also been installed near one stairway). They buy flowers, incense sticks, gold leaves and candles to offer at the pagoda from the stalls that line the stairs. (These stalls sell a variety of other things apart from religious objects.)

The atmosphere of the Shwedagon is steeped in the religious faith of the people who have worshipped there for generations. Everywhere are the sounds of prayers and the clear ring of prayer gongs. On the platform which surrounds the pagoda are many

People worshipping inside the Shwedagon pagoda in Rangoon—an important part of Burmese religious life

smaller pagodas, shrines and pavilions. Each person goes to his or her favourite place of worship to pray there and to make offerings. Apart from the main prayer pavilions, the eight planetary posts which mark the days of the week are popular places of worship. (Each day of the week, together with Rahu— Wednesday night—has its own planet.) People go to the post marking the day of their birth to pray, light candles and incense sticks and to make offerings of flowers and water. In a hot country like Burma, the coolness of water is symbolic of peace.

All Burmese know the day of the week on which they were born. The name given on a person's birth horoscope is decided according to the day of birth. For example, those born on a Monday should have names beginning with the letters *ka, hka,*

The planetary post which marks Rahu (Wednesday night). A particular animal—in this case, the elephant—is associated with each day of the week

ga, nga, those born on a Tuesday are given names beginning with *sa, hsa, za, nya,* and so on. Not just horoscope names but also those given by parents are usually chosen according to these rules. The horoscope shows the position of the planets at the time of a person's birth. Astrologers use it to make predictions about the future. This practice is not really in line with the teachings of the Buddha, according to which one's future is decided by one's own actions rather than by the stars.

Another side of Burmese life which is not strictly in accordance with Buddhist teachings is spirit-worship. Like the other peoples of Burma, the Burmese were spirit-worshippers before the arrival of Buddhism. The Burmese use the word *nat* to mean supernatural beings, the good ones who dwell in the various heavens as well as the frightening ones who interfere in the affairs of the human world. Little *nat* shrines can often be seen in Burma, especially under big trees which are believed to harbour spirits. The most powerful of all the *nats* are the *Thonzekhuna Min,* or "Thirty-Seven Lords". There are people who take *nat* worship very seriously in spite of their belief in Buddhism. Even

A *nat* shrine in a small village in the Shan State. Although it is not really in accordance with the teachings of Buddhism, spirit-worship is still widespread in Burma

those who avoid having anything to do with spirit-worship will not do anything which is known to be offensive to *nats*.

The most important place for *nat* worship in Burma is Mount Popa, an extinct volcano. Mount Popa is considered to be the home of two of the thirty-seven powerful *nats*. A great festival takes place there every year which attracts people from all over the country, *nat* worshippers as well as curious observers.

It is often asked why even educated Burmese can sometimes be found taking part in *nat* worship. Perhaps the answer lies in two aspects of Burmese life. One is the strong hold which old beliefs from the days before Buddhism still have on the minds of the people. The other is the extreme self-reliance which Buddhism demands from the individual. In Buddhism there are no gods to whom one can pray for favours or help. One's destiny is decided entirely by one's own actions. While accepting the

Mount Popa, the most important place for *nat* worship in Burma. There are a number of *nat* shrines on top of the extinct volcano

Celebrations for *Thingyan*, the Burmese New Year. This is also known as the Water Festival—for obvious reasons!

truth of this, most people find it difficult to resist the need to rely on supernatural powers, especially when times are hard.

The Burmese may put great importance on their religious life, but that does not stop them from being a fun-loving people. This is particularly obvious during the celebrations for the Burmese New Year, which takes place in April. *Thingyan* is also known as the Water Festival because the last three days of the old year are a time for people to throw water at one another all over the country. This is very refreshing at a time of year when the hot weather is at its worst. The water-throwing can sometimes get too rough, but nobody is supposed to get angry.

Thingyan is also a time when many Burmese boys celebrate one of the most important landmarks of their life. This is the

73

The *shinbyu* ceremony, at which the *shinlaung* is dressed in princely costume in remembrance of the fact that the Buddha was a prince before he gave up his position to follow a religious life

shinbyu, when a Buddhist boy enters the monastery for a short time as a novice monk. All Burmese parents see it as their duty to make sure that their sons are admitted to the religious life in this way. The *shinbyu* ceremony can be performed once the boy is old enough to say certain Buddhist prayers correctly, manage the robes of a monk, and ''drive away crows from his begging bowl''. This period of novicehood during which boys live the life of monks (although they do not keep all the rules which adult monks must observe) is a good introduction to the religious life. Burmese men like to enter monastic life at least three times during their lifetime: once as a boy, once as a young man and once as an adult.

The *shinbyu* ceremony is a joyful occasion. The candidate for

74

novicehood *(shinlaung)* is usually dressed in princely costume. This recalls the fact that the Buddha was a prince before he gave up his royal position to follow the religious life. The *shinlaung* is paraded through the streets with great ceremony before his head is shaved and he is given the robes of a novice. How simple or elaborate a *shinbyu* ceremony is depends on the inclinations and resources of the family. Often a number of boys take part in a single ceremony. Apart from the *Thingyan* period, the Buddhist Lent is a popular time for *shinbyu* ceremonies.

When brothers are having their *shinbyu,* it is usual for the sisters to have their ears pierced. This gives the girls a chance to dress up as princesses and have their share of fuss and

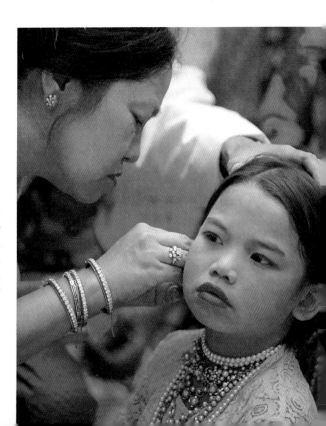

A Burmese girl having her ears pierced during her brother's *shinbyu* ceremony—this gives the girls an excuse to dress up as princesses and have their share of fuss and attention

attention. Many see this as an expression of the Burmese belief in the equality of men and women. Although, theoretically, men are considered nobler because only a man can become a Buddha, Burmese women have never really had an inferior status. They have always had equal rights of inheritance and led active, independent lives. Secure in the knowledge of her own worth, the Burmese woman does not mind giving men the kind of respectful treatment that makes them so happy!

A big *shinbyu* ceremony may be accompanied by a *pwe*. *Pwe* is a particularly Burmese word which can mean a festival, feast, celebration, ceremony, gathering or public performance. One common use of the word is to describe a popular entertainment which is a marvellous mixture of dance, drama, music and clowning.

The origins of Burmese dance are considered to go back at least to the Pagan period, judging from old wall paintings and references in stone inscriptions. However, many of the dances performed today owe a considerable amount to Thai influences introduced in the eighteenth century when a son of Alaungpaya brought back many artists from his invasions of Thailand. The movements of both male and female dancers are very graceful, involving beautiful hand gestures and extremely skilled footwork.

Burmese drama, which is a little like western opera with music, singing and much dramatic action, also owes a considerable amount to the tradition of court plays brought back from Thailand in the eighteenth century. Popular dramas such as the *Yamazat,* based on the famous Ramayana epic of India, are performed again and again. The nineteenth century produced many fine Burmese dramatists whose works also remain popular to this day.

Dance drama is always accompanied by orchestral music. Burmese musical instruments fall into five categories: bronze instruments, stringed instruments, leather instruments, hollow wind instruments, and non-metallic percussion instruments used for keeping time. Burmese orchestral music has a great range, from soft, gentle tones to the loud, stirring clashes which so often announce the presence of a *pwe.* The leading instrument of the orchestra is the *hsaingwaing,* a circle of twenty-one small leather-faced drums which are played with amazing virtuosity by the performer, who sits in the centre. Another instrument considered particularly Burmese is the gently curving harp, which is held in the lap of the performer as he plays.

There are many different types of classical Burmese song. To mention a few, there are the *kyo* (meaning ''string''), which is accompanied by stringed instruments; the *patpyo,* which is always preceded by little phrases of music on the *hsaingwaing;* and the *bawlè,* invented by a princess of the last royal dynasty at Mandalay.

Although classical music is always performed at the much loved *pwes,* modern music showing a strong western influence is increasingly gaining popularity, especially among young people. However, Burmese music and dance have not only strong traditions but also the support and encouragement of the

77

Dancing during the Water Festival. Although this dancer is not a professional, the grace and elegance of traditional Burmese dancing is still obvious

government. There is, therefore, little danger that they will fall into decline, in spite of modern developments.

One form of entertainment which has lost some of its popular appeal is the puppet show. This was first introduced in the late eighteenth or early nineteenth century for the amusement of the royal court. A traditional puppet show has twenty-eight characters, including *nats,* a king, queen, courtiers and various animals and birds. Different kinds of wood must be used to make

78

different characters. There are many other rules, such as the order in which the characters come on stage and the direction from which they emerge. Puppeteering is, therefore, a very specialized art. It is a great pity that the public no longer seem very interested in this fascinating form of entertainment.

Today, the cinema has much appeal for the Burmese. The Burmese film industry began before the Second World War. As in other countries, actors and actresses have many fans. But although successful film stars can make a good living, they do not become as rich as the big stars in the western countries. Traditionally, actors and dancers were considered an inferior class, but these old prejudices are fast disappearing. Television, which was introduced several years ago, is quickly gaining in popularity.

This type of harp is peculiar to Burma

The Burmese are an agricultural people, depending on the land for their living. Even today, in spite of some industries and the many professions open to people in the towns, agriculture is the backbone of the country. The number of those engaged in such professions as medicine, engineering and teaching is increasing all the time. The Burmese have always had a high proportion of people who could read and write. This is due to the custom of sending children to the local monastery for their schooling. Traditionally the monasteries limited themselves to religious teachings, but gradually more and more of them added modern subjects to their teaching programme. Nowadays, with the growth of state education, there are few monasteries serving as schools. However, there are still many Burmese who owe their early education to Buddhist monks.

It has already been mentioned that Burmese writing first began to develop in the Pagan period. Much of the traditional literature was concerned with religious themes. But there is also a considerable body of classical works, mainly verse, which deals with non-religious matters. Before the nineteenth century, the Burmese seem to have preferred poetry to prose. However, since the first novel in Burmese was published at the beginning of the twentieth century, prose writing, especially fiction, has developed greatly. Today, Burmese is a vigorous, continuously developing language.

The Burmese have a great respect for education. There is a popular old saying that riches can vanish as if by magic, but knowledge is a truly precious treasure which nobody can take

80

Three generations together—family ties are very important in Burma, and children are brought up to respect their elders

away. Traditionally, education was seen not just as the acquisition of knowledge but as the development of Buddhist values. The needs of the present age have led to more emphasis on formal qualifications, but parents still place importance on bringing children up as good Buddhists.

The family is very important in Burma. Children are brought up to honour and respect their elders. It is believed that the love and care given by parents are beyond repayment. Burmese are taught that even though the Lord Buddha showed his mother the way to *nirvana,* he did not manage to repay more than a minute portion of what he owed her.

In spite of the strong feelings of family, the Burmese do not have a system of family names. Each individual has his or her

81

own personal name, which is often quite different from those of everybody else in the family. Morover, women do not change their names on marriage. For example, the father may be called U Thein, the mother Daw Saw Tin, the son Maung Tun Aye, and the daughter Ma Khin Khin. *U, Daw, Maung* and *Ma* are prefixes like "Mr." or "Mrs.". In Burma, age is an important factor in deciding which prefix to use. *U* literally means "uncle" and *Daw* means "aunt", so these cannot be used for young children. *Maung,* meaning "younger brother", is suitable for a boy, but when he is older the prefix *Ko* ("older brother") will be used. However, *Ma* ("sister") is the only prefix used for girls. Sometimes it is the person's position that decides which prefix should be used. A young man who has achieved a very important position will be addressed as *U,* while an older man, if his status is low, may still be addressed as *Ko* or *Maung.*

A person's position may decide how much respect is shown to him, but Burmese society has no rigid class system. It is not possible to tell from a person's name or accent whether his father is a manual labourer or a wealthy businessman. Even his appearance is not always an indication of his background, as there is not a great deal of difference in the kinds of clothes people wear. Many of those who are in high positions come from humble homes. A person is judged by his own achievements rather than by his family.

An important part of Burmese life is food. Both Burmese men and women take a lively interest in cooking. The basic item of a Burmese meal is usually rice, taken with what westerners

82

Spices and chillis on sale in Taunggyi market. Spices, garlic and ginger are frequently used in Burmese cooking

would describe as a "curry". However, Burmese "curries" are not quite the same as the better known Indian ones. The Burmese use less spices but more garlic and ginger. Fish products are an important part of Burmese cooking. Fish sauce and dried shrimps are used for flavouring. *Ngapi,* a paste of preserved fish with a very strong smell, is taken as a relish at almost every meal. Meat is not eaten in large quantities. A great variety of vegetables is available all the year round and Burmese cooking makes full use of them. It has been said that no tender leaf or shoot is safe from the Burmese.

The numbers of Indians and Chinese in Burma have added further variety to the food of the country. In the towns there

83

are many restaurants and food stalls. It is quite usual for people to stop by the roadside to have a snack or a meal. Two of the most popular dishes are *mohinga* and *khaukswe*. *Mohinga* is a dish of slightly fermented rice noodles eaten with a thick fish soup. *Khaukswe* simply means noodles, and these can be prepared in many different ways. But the *khaukswe* dish considered most typically Burmese is the one eaten with a kind of chicken stew cooked in coconut milk.

In general, the Burmese do not eat many sweets. Hot, spicy snacks are more to their taste. Fruits often take the place of puddings. As in many other south Asian countries, the mango is very popular. There are many varieties and the Burmese eat them in a number of ways. Small green mangoes are taken with *ngapi* as part of the main meal, or eaten as a snack dipped in salt and chilli powder. Larger, slightly underripe mangoes can be made into a curry. But of course there is nothing to compare with a ripe, sweet mango eaten on its own.

Green tea is one of the most usual drinks in Burma. Tea with milk and sugar is also taken, but this is usually brewed in such a way that foreigners do not always recognize it as tea. As Buddhists, the Burmese frown upon alcoholic drinks, but there are strong country liquors made from the juice of the toddy palm. Bottled beer of the western variety is also produced nowadays.

Food is a popular subject of conversation. It is quite usual for friends and acquaintances to ask each other on meeting: "And what did you have for lunch today?". This constant interest makes Burmese cooking one of the most imaginative and varied in the world.

Both Burmese men and women wear the *longyi,* a long tube of cloth which they wrap around themselves and tuck in at the waist. Men wear western-style shirts with their *longyis* and women wear short, fitted tops. Young girls have now taken to wearing western-style blouses and T-shirts. For formal occasions, men wear collarless shirts with short jackets and a *gaungbaung* (a kind of turban) on their heads. Burmese women like to put flowers in their hair. Chains of sweet-smelling white jasmines coiled around a knot of glossy black hair is one of the most attractive sights. Traditionally, both Burmese men and women kept their hair very long. Men started to cut their hair soon after British rule was established in the country. However, men with large top-knots can still be seen in the villages. Women have continued to keep their hair long, but in recent years it has become fashionable for girls to adopt short, westernized hair-styles.

Burmese women are noted for their fine complexions. It is thought that they owe this in some degree to the use of *thanakha.* This is a paste made by grinding the bark of the *thanakha* tree. It gives the skin protection from the sun and is also thought to have medicinal properties. *Thanakha* is a yellow-beige paste and when applied thickly can make the face look as though it had been smeared with mud. In spite of this, it remains the most important item of a Burmese woman's beauty treatment. Even the arrival of modern cosmetics has not diminished the popularity of *thanakha.*

A busy market scene in Taunggyi. Most of the people in the photograph are wearing the traditional Burmese *longyi*

In Burma, as in many Asian countries, western goods are much sought after. Western ideas and attitudes have also crept in through books, films and foreign visitors. Under the policy of the present government, tourists are only allowed into the country for one week at a time. This goes some way towards keeping out foreign influences and, compared with most South-east Asian countries, Burma has done a much better job of preserving its own culture and traditions. The country is to some extent isolated from the rest of the world through restrictions on Burmese wishing to travel abroad as well as on foreigners wishing to come to Burma. This enforced isolation has resulted in giving things foreign the appeal of "forbidden fruit" for some Burmese. It also means that in many areas of scientific and

86

technological education, Burma has fallen behind modern developments.

Whatever attractions western goods and culture may hold for some of the Burmese people, Buddhism is still the greatest influence on their daily lives. Young people who dress in T-shirts and listen eagerly to western-style pop music still visit the pagodas frequently. The religious life of the Burmese is not separated from their social life. Most Burmese gatherings are centred around a religious event. The most common social occasion is perhaps the *hsoongway,* offering of food to monks. Friends will come to help, listen to the sermons and join in the chanting of prayers. It is usual to repeat the five precepts and undertake to keep them. On holy days people undertake to keep the eight precepts. After the monks have left, friends and family will eat together. It will have been an enjoyable as well as'a spiritually rewarding occasion.

By international standards, Burma is not a wealthy country and life is hard for many of its people. But there is still a quality of calmness and serenity which is very precious. For this the Burmese are greatly indebted to their religion.

Burmese Crafts

The only monuments and buildings of any great age in Burma are pagodas and monasteries. This is because the houses of ordinary people and even the palaces of kings were traditionally built from the various woods that are available in such abundance. Wooden buildings cannot survive for very long in the climate of Burma. The Burmese are skilled at working with wood. They use it not just for building but also for many decorative crafts.

Prayer pavilions at pagodas are often decorated with elaborate wood carvings. The Shwenandaw monastery in Mandalay boasts some of the finest carvings. It was originally within the grounds of the Mandalay palace. Fortunately King Thibaw had it moved outside, and thus it escaped when the rest of the palace complex was destroyed during the Second World War. The whole monastery is a feast of wood carvings: scrolls, flowers, animals and supernatural beings are arranged in a profusion of intricate patterns.

Almost every Burmese home has a shrine with one or more images of the Buddha. Often these images are placed on beautifully carved and gilt wooden thrones. Sometimes these thrones are lacquered or decorated with glass and mirror inlay. Gilt with glass inlay, known as *hman-si-shwe-cha,* is a well-known

88

decorative art. Some of the prayer pavilions of the Shwedagon show fine examples of this kind of work.

Images of the Buddha may be made of wood, marble or bronze. Some of the best images come from Mandalay and the surrounding districts. There is a good market for such images, as people are always setting up new shrines or adding to the old ones. Traditionally the Burmese were not interested in collecting antique images. In fact, some believe that it is unlucky to take into their homes old images which were once in pagodas or monasteries. The value which westerners put on antique goods is changing the attitudes of some Burmese. The smuggling of valuable old images is no longer uncommon. Many smuggled goods are sold over the border in Thailand.

Lacquerware is one of the most popular Burmese crafts. It is generally believed that the technique of lacquer originated in China. It was probably introduced to the Burmese when Anawratha's army brought back Mon craftsmen from Thaton. Burmese lacquer is slightly different from the Chinese and Japanese variety in that it is derived from a different species of the lacquer tree, *Melanhorroea usitata*. The sap of the tree is mixed with a special kind of ash and applied to a prepared base of wood, woven bamboo, or bamboo and horsehair. Enough of the mixture is applied to give a smooth surface before layers of coloured lacquer are applied.

There are several types of decorated lacquerware. The most common are incised lacquerware, gold-leaf lacquerware and relief-moulded lacquerware. In incised laquerware, designs are

Preparing an image of the Buddha for casting in bronze. Almost every Burmese home has a shrine with one or more images of the Buddha, and the manufacture of such images is a thriving craft

cut into the surface of an object. These designs are then filled in with coloured lacquer, the most usual colours being red, black, green and yellow. In gold-leaf lacquerware, gold-leaf decorations are applied to a black background. The decorations on relief-moulded lacquerware are made by modelling them in lacquer mixed with sawdust and ash, so that the designs are raised above the surface.

Bowls, trays, betel-nut containers and small decorative boxes are some of the most common items of lacquerware. Larger objects, such as tables and screens, are also made; but these can be very expensive.

The Burmese are skilled silversmiths. The most frequently

90

used item of silverware is the bowl. The slightly pot-bellied shape of the traditional Burmese bowl, which comes in many different sizes, is thought to be based on the begging bowls used by monks. Many of these bowls are embossed with scenes from Buddhist stories or from traditional Burmese court life.

On special occasions the Burmese like to wear their traditional hand-woven silk *longyis*. Those made with wavy or zig-zag designs in many colour combinations, called *acheik,* are considered the best fabrics. Of these *acheik,* the most rare and expensive are the ones woven with a hundred spools and therefore called *lun-taya (lun* means "spool" and *taya* means "one hundred"). The *lun-taya acheik* is thick and heavy and long-

A worker in a lacquerware factory in Pagan. Lacquerware is one of the most popular Burmese crafts

lasting. Such *longyis* are often passed down from generation to generation.

A Burmese craft which has practically died out is making embroidered wall hangings. It is thought that the inspiration and technique for these hangings came from India or from the west because of the name, *kalaga*. *Kala* is the Burmese term for foreigners from the west, and *ga* signifies a screen or curtain.

Although wall paintings can be seen in the monuments of Pagan, the Burmese have not really developed painting as a traditional art. Even the illustrations in folding books and manuscripts date back only to about the nineteenth century.

The best examples of Burmese art and crafts can be seen at religious monuments. This is a further indication of the importance of Buddhism in Burma.

A Common Future

In recent years a great deal of emphasis has been placed by foreigners on the rebellions against the Burmese government led by the Karens and the Shans, and the differences between the peoples of Burma have been pointed out. It has been implied that the nation is not a true union of peoples but an artificial state imposed from above. This record of disunity is not one of which any citizen of Burma can be proud. Nevertheless, there is more reason to be hopeful for the future than might appear to some observers.

There are many ties between the peoples of Burma. The Mon-Khmers, Tibeto-Burmans and Thai-Shans have lived among each other for centuries. The Mons and the Burmese, who were sworn enemies throughout much of their history, have learnt to live together in peace. With the development of mutual understanding and tolerance, the other peoples could also learn to live in harmony.

Burma's borders form a natural boundary for a country rich in peoples and natural resources. In time, both could be developed to create a strong and prosperous nation.

Index

95